Java L. Collins

A Letter
to My
Sisters:

An Awakening of Dreams

A *Letter to My Sisters:*
An Awakening of Dreams

Java L. Collins
ISBN: 1-882185-61-7
ISBN-13: 978-1-882185-61-0

Scripture quotations are taken from the King James Version of the Holy Bible.

Library of Congress Cataloging-in-Publication Data

Collins, Java L.
  A letter to my sisters: an awakening of dreams / by Java L. Collins.
    p. cm.
  ISBN 1-882185-61-7
1. African American women—Religious life. 2. Dreams—Religious aspects—Christianity.
3. Self-actualization (Psychology)—Religious aspects—Christianity. I. Title.

  BR563.N4C646 2005
  248.8'43—dc22

2005000485

Published by Cornerstone Publishing, Inc.
Wilmington, Delaware
www.cornerstonepublishing.com

Original Cover Illustration
by Andre Dandridge
Business Address:
Dandridge Designs
6023 Summerdale Avenue
Philadelphia, PA 19149
Business: 215-537-9331
E-mail: andredandridge@comcast.net

Revised Cover
by Nicole Blango
Business:
Precision Imaging Designs
Philadelphia, PA
ncatina6@aol.com

Java L. Collins

A Letter to My Sisters:

An Awakening of Dreams

Blessings, peace
& abundance!
Java

People who have no dreams always live in the broken places.

- Bishop T. D. Jakes

For my sisters,

for all those dreams

which have not

been fulfilled

. . . yet!

Acknowledgments

I want to take this time to thank my Heavenly Father for presenting this project to me, for blessing and amazing me by the doors He opens and the paths He sets before me every day.

To my son, Milton – I love you so much and thank God for the privilege of raising a son like you. Thank you for your words of encouragement and for believing in me.

To my sisters, Demetria, Sandra, Marguertia, Kimberly, Sonja, Dorothy, Sybil, and Viola – thank you for you all are incomparable as sisters and friends, also for being real and listening to me, even when you didn't want to, for loving me and allowing me to love you back.

To my brother, Stan – thank you for being my brother and my comic relief.

To Connie, Char, Jeanette, Cathy, Roslyn, Angie, Danieka, Vicki and Sonya – thank you for always being in my corner, my own personal cheerleaders.

To Autumn, Grace, Tanya, and Sharla – you are so remarkable, and I am so elated that God has connected us.

To Lisa, thank you so much for being real and having my back.

To Pastors Reggie and Candi Stewart, Isaiah, Lenora and Josh – thank you so much for opening up your home to me, loving me and treating me as part of your family. I love you so much!

To Pastor Èmil and Lisa Hawkins, Pastors Ray and Tracey Barnard, Liberty World Outreach and Impacting Your World Ministries – thank you so much for imparting and impacting my life!

To my new family, Pastor Stephen Rathod and Covenant Family Church – thank you so much for welcoming me in and covering me at the time I needed it most!

To all my other sisters, this is for you, and my prayer is that I can continue to contribute positively to your lives for countless years to come.

jlc

Sisterhood: A Legacy

Fighting, slapping fives,
Bonding, hanging,
Connecting, protecting.
Sometimes hating,
Sometimes slandering, gossiping,
Loving . . . are we.
Sisters.

You see, sisterhood isn't something you're just born into,
It's not something you just be.
But sisterhood is about us, women; it's about you and me.
Real sisters.

Uptown, downtown, all around the town.
Shopping, mopping, moping, frowning.
Laughter, tears, pain, shame.
Hustling, bad men, good men, playing games.
It's all the same – surviving.
Real sisters.

Being real.
If it's one thing sisters know – it's about being real.
It's the being "real" that makes us go to the uttermost depths
for each other.
It's the being "real" that makes us feel,
That touches us deep within our souls, our hearts, our beings.
Men . . . take note, to get to a sister - you gotta be real.
It makes us hang tight, when times get tough.

It makes us fight, when we want to give up.
It makes us strong, when we feel like crying.
Sisters.
Real sisters.

See, sisters are there for each other.
In good times, bad times,
Rain, snow, storms,
Hey, any kind of weather.

We fall in,
We fall out.
But our love still remains. . . .
honest, tight, true . . .
but most of all real.

Sisterhood, it's a bonding,
a thing that creates legacies . . . a woman thang.

Sisterhood, yeah, I am a part of it,
and sister, I want you to know,
I am here for you,
You are here for me.

We're here to see each other through, not just to be.
There's nothing we can't get through – you and me, me and you.
True, you'll make me mad, and I will do the same to you,
But know this, sister, you can't get rid of me.
Sisters. Yeah.
Real sisters.

- *Java L. Collins*

Contents

Chapter   *Page*

Introduction 25

1   A Time to Dream 31
2   A Time to Mourn 37
3   A Time to Look Around 43
4   A Time to Survive 49
5   A Time to Discover 55
6   A Time to Speak 59
7   A Time to Choose 63

Poem: *My Soul Desire* 67

8   A Time to Gain Strength 71
9   A Time to Heal 75
10   A Time for Challenges 81
11   A Time to Be Awakened 87
12   A Time to Laugh 93
13   A Time to Love 99
14   A Time to Embrace 105
15   A Woman Unfinished 111

Poem: *Unlock My Soul* 119

Foreword

Java L. Collins has captured the heart cry of women all over the world. Her unique experiences give her a glimpse into various situations sisters have shared themselves. This book will begin a process of restoring relationships that have been broken. Read this, examine yourself, and ask what is the part you play, between your sisters, you and your dreams.

Reginald J. Stewart, M. Div.
Assistant Pastor
Impacting Your World Christian Center
Philadelphia, Pennsylvania

Preface

Success is about maintaining the vision even through the most grueling details.

- Paul Newby, Designer, TiVo, Inc.

As a child I struggled with being teased about being a dreamer. Recently, I heard Pastor Jentezen Franklin say that a dreamer is the one who holds the promises of God. I boldly carry the title of a dreamer now, because God has allowed me to be one of many whom He has chosen to hold His promises. Often I succumbed to the enemy whenever he sent assassins to take my dream — assassins in the form of low self-esteem, doubts, unbelief and feelings of unworthiness.

My journey began with the big question of "*If you could do anything in the world and not worry about money, what would it be?*" When I wrote this book, I was going over my life doing a personal inventory and identifying areas where I needed to make some major changes. Little did I know that at the same time, God was revealing to me that I could not witness to others about someone else's life story that I must use my own life story, and that my story is HIStory.

It is my heart's desire to fulfill my purpose in life, as well as to help you achieve and fulfill your purpose in life. Our purposes are often tied to our dreams. If you are ignoring the dream, then you are probably ignoring your purpose. These are dreams, which we have buried, or placed on the back burner until a more opportune time as we travel through life feeling unfulfilled, without understanding why. It is my desire to inspire you to begin to your search for your dream.

Of the people I have met, only a small percentage are living their dreams. The others are living the "nightmare." They have dreamed one thing but are living something else. After talking with them, I realized that I was one of those in the mainstream not living my dream and decided that I would not go another year pursuing something that would not bring me peace and fulfillment.

Thus the purpose of this book is to bring freedom, enlightenment, and hope. We are not bound to our past, but it does serve a purpose.

Our past is not to be used as an excuse or crutch for not pursuing our purpose; however, since we cannot change the past, let us utilize it by using it to build the foundation of your purpose. Remember, you cannot tell someone else's story; it must be your own, for you have not lived someone else's life. Use this book to give you that extra push you need to live your dreams. It is your life and you should be living it.

Life is a big ripple, and we all play a part in someone's life. When you throw a rock into the water, it creates a ripple, which in turns produces another ripple, and so on. You are a ripple in the pond. Whether you believe it or not, we are connected to one another. There is a chance that you may be the link to helping someone else fulfill his or her dream.

There are four goals for someone who is reading this book:

1) for you to realize that in order to pursue your dream you must be willing to be stripped of your ideology, feelings, your way of how you think things must go before your dream can come to pass;

2) you will go through a period where you will feel dry, dusty, alone, like someone has knocked you into a pit and left you there;

3) recognize that everyone you meet or know is not called to help you along in your dream process; and

4) is for you to catch a dream, awaken to you purpose, write the vision, and fly with it, no longer looking back and regretting. For your ears to perk up, excitedly as you begin to write out and visualize your dream.

As you read this book, you will find that the use the words *dream, vision, and purpose* are interchangeable. I want you to focus on this definition as you read:

Purpose: finding and doing what you love, increasing your chances of being able to accomplish what God has placed you here to do.

Hebrews 10:24 states that you and I are to "*consider one another, to provoke unto love and to good works.*" God calls us to thoroughly weigh one another and pay careful attention to each other, being accepting one's self and one another as accepted by God. This frees us up to discover each other's dreams as well as to learn to care for one another.

One of the questions I asked before putting this to paper was: "*God, who am I to be influencing with this book? What do you want accomplished through me as I pursue my own dream?*" As you pursue your dream, ask God for the questions that you need to build your own foundation.

As you begin to hit stumbling blocks and go through trials, let it serve as confirmation to you that the enemy is convinced that your dream is coming to pass. And once the dream gets inside of you and you begin to embrace it, then the dream will become greater than the enticement to not pursue it.

My prayer is for this book to bless you, empower you to change, to dream, and to help others do so as well. May God be with you on this journey.

- *Java L. Collins*

There is a time for everything,

And a season for every activity

under heaven:

A time to be born and

a time to die,

A time to plant and

a time to uproot,

A time to kill and

a time to heal,

A time to tear down and

a time to build,

A time to weep and

a time to laugh,

A time to mourn and

a time to dance,

A time to scatter stones and

a time to gather them,

A time to embrace and

a time to refrain,

A time to search and

a time to give up,

A time to keep and

a time to throw away,

A time to tear and

a time to mend,

A time to be silent and

a time to speak,

A time to love and

a time to hate,

A time for war and

a time for peace.

- Ecclesiastes 3:18 (NIV)

part I

A Time to Dream

A Time to Mourn

A Time to Look Around

A Time to Survive

A Time to Discover

A Time to Speak

A Time to Choose

INTRODUCTION

My Dearest Sisters,

Hope sees the invisible,

Feels the intangible, and

Achieves the impossible.

- Anonymous

The Scriptures state there is a time for everything, for every season and activity under the heavens, which more or less translates to mean, my Sisters, this is your time to seek out your season.

People are dying today for something new. What we fail to understand is we must be able to comprehend the old in order to understand the new. Sometimes, the new is actually the old being rediscovered. So it can be with dreams, purposes, and passions.

The definition for *new* is *"of recent origin; appearing for the first time."* When the Bible speaks of a new creation, it is speaking of *"consistently being changed,"* evolving into being more than what you are at this present moment. You have got to yearn for something better if you want to do better. One of my goals is to be an inspiration to the people around me. There is a desire instilled in me to encourage and motivate others to do better. In order to improve, you must prepare and you must be willing to take the risks!

It was probably ten years ago, when I realized I was not fulfilling the dreams, which stirred in my heart. Though, I was good at encouraging and motivating others to pursue their dreams, their purpose, their passion, I seemed helpless to do this for myself. I kept taking jobs thinking this would satisfy me, although I knew it was not what I wanted to do.

My turning point came three years ago, when I made the decision to take another executive administrative position, even after praying to God and specifically stating that I wanted to go a different route. I took the position thinking for some reason, that this would be different and I would be launched into an area where I would find fulfillment. The position lasted less than a year, and I, once again, began to contemplate what my next move would be. I pondered the possibility that perhaps God was trying to move me closer towards my destiny, but I was being mulish and stubborn.

After fasting and praying, I heard the voice of the Lord say, *"You are in the best season of your life."* I remember bursting into laughter and saying, *"God, how can that be? I do not have a job!"* Then it seemed almost everywhere I turned there were letters, or reminders of what I always said I would do *"one day."* But as we all know, *"one day"* never comes, if you do not make time for it.

As the prospect of obtaining gainful employment looked bleak, I decided to take a risk. After all, I had nothing to lose. I felt a prompting to call my father and stepmother and ask if I could come and stay for a moment, which they readily told me yes. It turned out to be one of the most mind blowing and eye opening decisions I had ever made in my life!

During my stay I was able to bring closure to some thoughts, doubts, questions and issues, or whatever you want to call it; not only in my relationship with my father, stepmother and siblings, but I was able to release some baggage which I had been carrying around in life. Then, viola! I realized it was the excess baggage, which kept me from pursuing my dreams and my passions. My process of sorting through each piece of baggage individually, setting aside the pieces, deciding what to keep and what to get rid of because I was not ready to throw very much away yet.

This acknowledgment brought me to a point of peace and stability by creating an atmosphere for me to see a clearer picture of whom I really am and what I was created to do. As this picture began to form, I had a very liberating feeling begin to stir in my soul. Though, I still had baggage to unload and stages to proceed through, I was starting the first leg of my journey to dream, and in order for me to dream I realized I had to change.

Life changes will not happen all at once. They are developed in stages, which will help create a healthier us as we strive for our dreams. These changes will only become permanent if we want them to be. I love those commercials that encourage us to do it for the loved ones in our lives. However, the actuality is if we will not do it for ourselves, generally, we will not do it for someone else. So therefore, we cannot expect to change for our families, our husbands, our children, our mothers, our fathers, but we must want do to it for ourselves. We must come to the realization that we are important. We must come to understand what our speeds are, what our styles are, and aim for the changes which are always on the horizon. As Pastor Cynthia Brazelton said one time, "*You have got to see your ship come sailing in.*" See, your ship, it is on the horizon making its way in!

Maya Angelou, in her book, "*Wouldn't Take Nothing for My Journey Now,*" says:

"*Each of us has the right and the responsibility to assess the roads which lie ahead, and those over which we have traveled, and if the future road looms ominous or unpromising, and the roads back uninviting, then we need to gather our resolve and carrying only the necessary baggage, step off that road into another direction. If the new choice is also unpalatable, without embarrassment, we must be ready to change that as well.*"

Do you understand? If the road you are on is not satisfying, change your direction, your path. When you dare to pursue your dreams, my Sisters, you must prepare yourself for the changes, which will happen, in your life. You must be prepared to enter a time of transition, where nothing will seem stable. Where you will speak and cry out to the Lord, yet at times, hear nothing but stillness.

In order to pursue your purpose, know this: The sin from your past will present itself as an obstacle to block you. You must remind yourself that neither man nor the enemy can shred up the evidence of your sins, but God can and will do so. Then in His love, God justifies you, forgives you, and scrubs you clean. Do not allow yourself to stay in bondage, or in company with the mindset that will hold you hostage by saying: "I can't! It's too hard! I don't have time! I'm not good enough!" These are all saboteurs of the dream or purpose that has been placed inside you by God.

In Romans 5:17, it says: "*For if by one man's offence death reigned by one; much more they which receive abundance of grace and of the gift of righteousness shall reign in life by one, Jesus Christ.*" Through this Scripture, you will get a point of release to live your life "*on purpose.*" Christ died for you to have abundant life, for you to live your life on purpose. Determine in your heart you do not want to miss opportunities presented by God anymore.

In quiet times, you will learn to encourage yourself by writing yourself notes, quotes, Scripture verses and placing them around you at home and work, and by developing a relationship with God. Galatians 5:16 state, "*This I say then, Walk in the Spirit, and ye shall not fulfill the lust of the flesh.*" When you have the Word before you continually, it makes it a little more difficult for the enemy to come in and wreck havoc.

Once you make the choice to find your dream and fulfill it, you are at war with "*who you are now*" versus "*who you are really meant to be.*" It is God's desire for you to know your true self, to begin the process of building your life. You do not want what you **have not done** to play a constant scenario in your mind, a stream of unfinished "what ifs." Though, I had toyed with this book for over seven years, I believe now I have entered the season for its release. We have all traveled different paths of life. We have all struggled in one sense or another. There is a time of release in the air, is it now for you? Is it your time? Your season?

There is such a level of compassion in me to reach out to all, especially my Sisters, blood and otherwise. To let you know, you can still pursue your dream and be a woman, a wife, a mother, a daughter, an aunt, a grandmother, and a career person. I encourage you to no longer let what you do stop, define, or keep you from being who you are meant to be!

Chapter 1
A Time To Dream

Go confidently

in the direction

of your dreams!

Live the life

you've imagined.

- Henry David Thoreau

One of my favorite lines is from a Disney cartoon in which Cinderella sings, "A *dream is a wish your heart makes.*" This is for you, my Sisters. I believe that dreams can serve to enlighten you, which makes them very precious jewels. Make a wish, regardless of where you are, the color of your skin, being young or old, the circumstances and situations you face, or the religions you practice. This is for you. This is your time. To help you see again, hear again, listen again, speak again, love again, laugh again, live again, but most of all . . . to dream again.

When I was younger, my mother would let my sisters and I sleep outside. Those were the days when it was safe and you knew no one would come in your backyard and do something stupid. On those nights we would lay our blankets on the warm, soft grass and look up into the sky, laughing, and giggling in hushed tones about what we wanted to be. Then we would spot the brightest star and say:

> *Star light, star bright,*
> *First star I see tonight,*
> *I wish I may, I wish I might*
> *Have my dreams come true tonight.*

One of my sisters wanted to become a lawyer, another wanted to be marry a pastor and have him become a Supreme Court Justice; another wanted to be an astronaut; another wanted to become a world famous fashion designer and I wanted to dance, while righting the injustices done to the underdog. We would laugh and talk of the things we wanted to be and the places we wanted to go. Our dreams were so real and they mattered. And to my host of other ethnic sisters, I say, no matter what your dreams are they do matter.

With the eyes of a child, we saw how big a dream could be. With awesome wonder, we began to realize how big the universe could be, and began to think, know, believe, and feel that nothing could stop us from achieving our dreams, our goals, our passions. We weren't afraid to dream, while actually believing with all of our hearts those dreams would come true.

Then something happens along the way on this road called life. Perilous, dangerous stops and pitfalls were hidden along the way, some visible, others invisible. Some have even taken the lives of our precious sisters. There will be times when you will wish you had never been born. And other times still when you wish the earth would open up and swallow you, or if you believe in God, wish for Jesus to return right now.

Life. You have heard about it, read about it and, up until this point you have experienced it. But yet, nothing quite prepares you for it. You spend most of it wondering, guessing, imagining, and even dreaming of how much better life would be for you once you got older and wiser, yet nothing happens. One might view it as a strange twist of fate, which sends you along a spiraling ride to destinations which most of the time are unknown. Many times events in life will crush your spirits, as well as whatever you attempt to attain.

Your opponents will knock you down, trample on and over you, and yes, even spit on you. Their actions say they do not value the contributions you have made. The battles, the wars, even the little skirmishes, leave you on the battlefield — bruised, battered and worn, the worst for wear. These curves of life have changed your hopes, your dreams, and your life. I am writing to you to let you know I feel your hurt; I see your pain. I realize and understand about having a broken heart from unfulfilled dreams . . . for I am a sister, too.

As you desperately try to make things work out, whether it is to try putting food on the table, make ends meet, or put up with a mate (you know, the one you are trying to change, the one that will not fit into your mold). This is why my heart bleeds and cries out to you and for you, my Sisters, because I love you and it hurts me to see you there, in those places. I want to see you set free, living . . . living . . . living!

I know life has not been fair to you or to me, but you cannot just stop living . . . or can you? Sometimes you will choose to let life pass you by. Hanging on day in, day out; never allowing THAT dream to enter your mind, or come forth. You deny yourself the joy, the opportunity, the privilege to get a glimpse of your REAL self. You push it away as if it is contagious. You do so by choice, using for excuses how you feel, how you were raised, or even the circumstances and situations in your life, even to the point of twisting the Word of God to support your excuse.

You do have a choice, a decision to make. Yes . . . yes . . . yes, your environment, your childhood, your experiences shaped your life, but you STILL have the ability to make a CHOICE, good or bad, right or wrong. You are all part of the same vision, of which each of us holds a different piece of the dream. Your dreams are tied to your life. They are a part of you.

At times, they have sustained you, becoming part of your unconscious focus. The traumas of unfulfilled dreams can have a devastating assault on your life; they can cripple you, leave you abandoned, and in some instances, even kill you. Proverbs 13:12 say "*hope deferred makes the heart sick.*" You are dragging around feeling unsure, unaware because your heart is sick from not fulfilling your potential, your worth, and your dream.

For so long you have been taught to act upon what others have said to you. This is where you have learned to place your value, respect and expectations. Whether the words came from a parent, teacher, and leader in the community, church or someone whose opinion that you have placed high value on. Now is the time to be truthful to yourself.

A lot of decisions I have made were based on what would make others happy and not me. I am learning that by choosing my dream, I am the one responsible for it. Yet, I know as well that my choice to pursue my dream will affect those around me. I made a conscious effort to pursue my dream. When I did, I became more confident, stronger, capable and responsible. And I know that once you purpose to pursue what is in you, you will become more confident and focused in your life.

You will begin to stop looking for approval from others. Please understand, I am not saying go buck wild and drop all of your current responsibilities (i.e. husband, family, work). I am saying I believe God can make a way for you to incorporate your dream into your current situation.

Your dream should make you seek and search for yourself, for who you are really meant to be. You should embrace change, just like the autumn leaf changes with the turn of the season. The nature embraces the warmth and welcomes the change. It represents a constant, steady element, bringing with it an expected sense of harmony, which creates a unique balance in the human structure of the arena of life.

The completion of a dream can be a symbol of a season ending or beginning, only to begin again, to fulfill other dreams. You need to grasp that good things are allowed to happen to you, and are supposed to happen to you, but regardless, you must realize someone has got to make it happen and that someone is you!

It is interesting that long ago there was an old adage, which said, "*If mama ain't happy, then nobody's happy*" and it seemed to be a fact. Yet you push your unhappiness aside and hide behind the mask as you struggle to produce an expression of agreement and bliss. I say, "*It is time to make mama happy again.*"

It is time to begin to weep and mourn over those things that have hindered you, and be less frantic about schedules, time pressured events, and running here and there. You must begin to focus on your God-given purpose, as if your life depends on it. My Sisters, embrace the new, which God has prepared for you; embrace the preparation time to birth your dream. Take a deep breath and prepare to jump into your purpose!

Chapter 2
A Time To Mourn

I'm doing better than good

and better than most

and sometimes

even better than that.

I'm great and getting better.

- Anonymous

Upon remembering the day my mother died I realized just how ineffective I felt. It was as though someone had just drained me of all energy and life. The bottom had dropped out of my world. I had lost my mother and my best friend. Yet, I put on my mask and pretended everything was all right. *"God would see us through! Hallelujah!"*

My mother had been dead for eleven years before I finally allowed myself the freedom to mourn her passing and what she had meant to me. I finally felt it was okay to hurt and grieve because she was not with me anymore. Letting myself finally feel the deep cutting that death can bring. Remembering the pain and how I thought it would never end.

Oh, my Sisters, with that same fervor is how I yearn to take you in my arms, like a mother takes a child, soothe your troubles away, your broken heart, and your fears. Letting you know that everything will be all right. How I wish I could make perfect your life. No hardships. No failures. No troubles. No faults. No wrongs. No broken hearts. No lost loves. No heartaches. No pains. No tears. . . just perfect in spirit, in being, in love, and in life.

My Sisters, my Sisters, my Sisters, by now you are asking yourself where did I go wrong? What has taken me to this offbeaten path? Away from your dreams. Away from yourself. Away from your joy, your laughter, your passion. Away from life.

Did those teachings and advice from your elders fall on deaf ears? As you grew, you thought you knew it all, thinking more highly of yourself than you should. Now, you feel trapped and isolated, placed in a horrible dungeon, someplace in your life – out . . . of . . . control. Spiraling down once again in this great abyss called life, leaving yet another dream unrealized and unfulfilled. And leaving you very distant from it, losing touch once more. Distancing yourself from your passions, your dreams that represent you.

God wants you to have life, my Sisters. A life so complete. A life so abundant. A life so vibrant. A life so overflowing. Even when you are squirming in the pits of darkness, or wallowing in the murky mud of self pity, there is hope!

So often when you speak and your words come back to you void, empty, and so full of despair, pity, and hopelessness. Some of you indulge yourself on having a pity party! And would like to invite guest if you could. While some have survived the tumultuous season, churning on the inside, and a few have looked at life and abandoned it and dropped out. Others have lost their lives to the storms, which have raged deep within.

Yet, when your dreams die, so do your visions. It sends your mind on a neverending quest to find God. IF there is a God, why doesn't He do something? IF there is a God, where is He? IF there is a God, when is He going to stop by and see about me? IF there is a God, how is He going to help me? IF there is a God, what is He going to do to help me? IF He loves me so much, then why is He letting this happen to me? To my family? Why? Why? Why? (*How about a little cheese with that whine?*)

It is this cry, echoing through your mind, your heart, your being. You feel more trapped than loved. Why? You have lost sight of your dream and have no clue as to what it looks like. What does your dream sound like to you? You feel stifled, confused, and lost. You feel abandoned by God. You become bored, brainwashed, subjected to the life that you have become accustomed to living; and right now. . . . you are not happy people.

If God loves you, why do you feel so trapped, so unloved, and so miserable? If God is so able, why are you in so much pain? If God is so able, why are you hurting? If God is so able, why are you, especially those who follow Him, so miserable? (*Want a little more cheese with that whine?*)

With these questions, it makes it easy for the enemy to have you play the blame game, in which God becomes the scapegoat along with others, making everyone to blame but you. In part, your history has taught you to do this. Ah, and it is a lesson you have learned very well. A lesson that you are unknowingly teaching your children and your children will teach their children, who in turn will teach their children and so on, unless the cycle is destroyed.

You get frustrated when your dreams elude you. As you ineffectively try to gain momentum, and figure out how to make the dream work or how to revive it, by and on your own terms of course, you become increasingly more frustrated. Your discouragement increases, while your faith decreases. (*Still whining? Have a little more cheese.*)

But now, the time to rise up has come. It is time to stop this foolishness, this madness. The time for change has come to stop the cycle from repeating. Your focus is to change your history, and reset the course of your destiny, your purpose, your dreams, and your visions.

God is love, and His true love knows no limits. So then, why are you limited? Why do you not soar, but cower in the shadows of darkness? You have a yearning, a hungering, and an overwhelming desire to go toward and be in the light? Why, oh, why do you sit with abated breath, while watching others take flight? Wishing you had the boldness to go forth and be the conquerors God has called you to be.

What I am trying to say is that most of you, my Sisters, at one point and time in your life, have put your dreams on hold for whatever reason and have left them there. I believe **now is the time to take back your dream.** Look at the excuses you have made that have kept you where you are, and then scatter those issues to the wind. Dust off your dream and breathe life back into it.

And for you, my Sisters, who have never had this problem, praise God! Perhaps you can be support for those of us who are struggling to find our dreams, our place in life.

Chapter 3
A Time
To Look Around

You have to expect

things of yourself

before you can do them.

- Michael Jordan

One of my favorite fairy tales is the one called *Stone Soup*. In the story, a man puts a pot of water on a fire to boil and puts a stone in it. By and by various people come by and each makes a contribution to the soup. Well, in the end they end up with a great tasting soup and had enough to feed everyone.

I love this story because it resembles life at times, where everyone can make a contribution – good or bad – it soon overloads you and begins to be stored up, thereby causing a little something extra being put in your "soup," changing its flavor, changing you.

In your relationships, you make excuses for your children, husband, friends, other siblings ... and sometimes yourself, to justify your happenings and circumstances. Giving you a reason to keep your bad tasting soup. Constantly, consciously and unconsciously, trying to prove that you are happy being weighed down. You begin to believe it for so long that it becomes a fact and you never reflect on how this makes you "really" feel. Faking the funk – faking the love, the care, and the concern. Sometimes, what someone else has looks a lot better than what you have.

So you begin to compare to your relationships – family, acquaintances, friends, enemies, people who are familiar with and to you – with others to create justification, for your sense of belonging, while unknowingly falling short of achieving your dream. This is due in part because you insist on making comparisons among those who are very familiar with your ways. They come into your home and are really at home — using things, borrowing things, constantly talking about the changes they would make in your home. Their talk fills your mind, not of how to fulfill lost dreams, but of endless chatter that has no real meaning. You begin to think that you are like them, while all the time God is saying otherwise. You look to some of the relationships you have formed and feel like something is always lacking. There is no joy there. And now, the pretense of joy takes too much energy and too much time, and life is still drifting by leaving you still in yesterday's state.

In some relationships, whether male or female, you feel so locked into this relationship

that you do not know how to get out. You can be tied into others by guilt, obligation, nothing better to do, or even feel that this is your destiny in life. You may even feel an urging to get out of that relationship, but never pay that urge any heed.

These relationships make you feel more "trapped" than loved. Why? Because for most of us, we do not know what love looks like or what it sounds like. There are times you feel stifled and abandoned by God. You become bored, which leads you to finally recognize that you have become a very unhappy person.

And my Sisters, why do most of our relationships with men end up leaving us the worst for wear? We as women must learn to stop seeing our men, our brothers, as our knights in shining armor, as our saviors. We need to stop believing the myth that once we hook up with them everything will be all right, because it will not be this way. If it was not right before we got together, it will not be right afterwards. Two broken halves do not make a whole. I am not male bashing, but just viewing our life situations for what they are.

NOW as you look at your life, your family, your friends, your relationships . . . you can now begin to wonder about the truth, the REAL truth, the GLORY of GOD truth. This is a phase of scattering stones, or in other words, facing issues. It is about opening up the excess baggage and taking inventory of what you have packed. This journey is about taking a look at what you need and do not need for it.

Go back to the time of your first "real kiss" – how your heart fluttered as your lips brushed his lips, which felt so warm and soft like feathers. His touch was so sweet, so passionate it lingered for hours and with it, he knew that he had you body, soul, and spirit. You gave yourself away so freely . . . with reckless abandon . . . so easily . . . that at times it frightened you, perplexed you, but somehow it NEVER ceased to release you from its captivity, nor did you want it to. This is the passion I want you to use to chase your dream.

You wonder, you think, you ponder, you have searched your thoughts — he used to love you so much, now what has happened? What did you do wrong? Where did you go wrong? You feel manipulated, pressured, and worn out. These feelings, more often than not, leave you empty and unsatisfied.

I remember my ex-husband and how I loved him and would have done anything for him, and did. I let my love blind me to the abuse I received from him emotionally and physically. When he would abuse me, I would view it as something I had done, and therefore deserved the abuse. It left me unsatisfied, helpless and hopeless about my situation. The thought that I was used and damaged goods filled my mind and I abandoned any idea of finding someone to love me again. And somehow I did, I found love in myself. Now, I can easily pray for him and forgive him, as well as forgive myself.

We all grow at different levels and stages. How often have you loved, whether kin or not, only to recall their fears, their lies, their betrayal of your love for them? How they focused on your destruction, instead of encouraging you to be all that you could be and still can be, encouraging you to fly . . . high . . . higher . . . to your highest heights.

The desire is to have someone in your life, which will see you as an equal, while supporting you as you are pursuing your dream. Someone whom you can share your life with, not as one who can come in and dominate your life, taking it over without any regard to who you are, what you need, or what you desire.

Our strength and love for our men should not demean them, but affirm them. It should not be to see how they satisfy us sexually, but as a "whole" being. What we do and mean to each other should last a lifetime and not until divorce court. We should learn to see them as a companion, a friend, a confidant, a husband, a father, a leader, and a lover. Not becoming consumed with them or their needs, but with the desire to fulfill one another needs as one. Just as we represent one in the Body of Christ, when it comes to fulfilling your dream, you should seek and find wise counsel (Proverbs 1:5) to become one with.

As you scatter the stones of your life, even your relationships, you will stumble into a void left by those stones while climbing the mountain searching for who you are. Searching for fulfillment that will not elude you, that will not betray you, that will bring God all the glory.

Chapter 4
A Time To Survive

Nothing outshines a woman

who dares to be herself.

- Angle S. Bush

The night air was balmy. Diamonds in the shape of stars lighted the sky. I stood in the quiet on the mountainside, staring at the water as it beckoned me to come in for a swim. Its dark shades with hints of white foam played in the moonlight. A mesmerizing sight to behold. Suddenly, I was airborne. I dove into the invitingly cool water.

As I swam, I somehow got off course and ended up near some seaweed. I tried to swim over it, but my left foot got caught. I went underwater to pull myself free, and then my right foot got caught. The more I struggled to free myself from the seaweed, the more it entangled me, and engulfed me to the point it had almost overtaken me. I was struggling to live, to survive.

Then I woke up.

****

Life can be like a reflection of this dream. It can create situations or circumstances, which may cause you to struggle to survive.

God ordains life, relationships, and even circumstances, but when things are out of order, it overwhelms you as you struggle against it. Even though some of these struggles are from your own choosing, they possess the potential to overtake WHO you are and your purpose. Then no matter how painful and no matter what the cost, it is time to let go. You must come to realize and accept this fact:

> *"THERE ARE PEOPLE IN YOUR LIFE*
> *WHO CANNOT FULFILL CERTAIN NEEDS*
> *THAT YOU HAVE."*

You must realize you are not here to unceasingly meet an unmet need of someone you know and/or love. Nor are you here to always protect others from harsh realities. You are here to develop, pursue, grow and be true to your God-given purpose, which involves helping others, not crippling them, encouraging them, and not destroying them.

There are times, my Sisters, if you are honest with yourself, you will admit that you would like to walk away from the whole ball of wax — family (children included, though this is NOT to say that you do not love them), friends, jobs, church, and work. Walk away and never look back and never think twice about what you have left behind.

The regrets, the faults, the bills, the failures in and of your life are what the enemy uses to constantly and consistently defeat you. He uses these lies to pull you down into the murky gorge of despair, depression, defeat, with no hope of triumph, and no victory in sight. You become like a condemned person on death row, awaiting a reprieve. You stand waiting for someone else to give you back your life.

LIFE. Most of the time you treat it so casually or carelessly, waiting for it to drop presents, good times, etc. into your lap. You desire the perfect life. The perfect spouse. The perfect children. The perfect job. The perfect house. The perfect income. The perfect car. The perfect neighborhood. The perfect attitude or personality. The perfect friends. And so on and so on. Then you get despondent and depressed when it did not arrive yesterday, and you realize your life is not perfect!

While playing the victim role, you begin to wonder and cry out. When? When? Oh, when? As you begin to think or believe no one has heard your cry. You are all alone. No one knows or can understand what you are going through. No one is there to help. You feel lost and all alone, spiraling down into the dark gulf of life.

All this time you please, you give, and you share so much of yourself with others, that there is nothing left for you. The more you strive to create a balance, the more unbalanced you seem to become. It is like walking a tightrope, or walking on eggshells or dangling in thin air, with barely enough energy to hang on.

You have so many people — family, friends, acquaintances, who are constantly pulling on you. They stand confused and helpless when you have no more to give them. Then the voice in you, says aloud, "What is wrong with me? Why can't you help me?" Not knowing that you have reached the end of your rope. No more solutions, no more advice, no more dreams, no more life. You now beg the darkness to swallow you up, as everything now seems hopeless. (*Need more cheese with that whine?*)

Hopelessness. Hopelessness. My Sisters, you forget there is a light at the end of the tunnel, though it seems so dim and distant, ever growing cold and faint. The light seems as if it is moving further and further away. There is no hope left in you. You have no desire, no dream to spend the rest of your life in the projects or in subsidized housing. You take two steps forward, only to seem like you have been pushed ten steps back. You are where you dreaded being, just like Job . . .

Struggling . . .
Struggling . . .
STRUGGLING!
Drowning . . .
Drowning . . .
DROWNING!
Soon it grows dark . . .
Darker . . .
Darkest . . .

and it turns into . . . . DARKNESS!

You are on the verge of selfdestructing! It is time to begin a new search before you destroy

other precious lives, including your own. You strive for everything to be so perfect. I say, "*Stop striving for man's form of perfectionism!*" The type of perfectionism you are searching for cannot be found in the flesh. In Romans 12:2, Paul tells us not to conform to this world but to pursue the perfect will of God. So what you seek is found in the will of God.

God wants you to have revelation in your walk, in your family, in your service, in your life! Be truthful to yourself. Determine that you want to do what pleases God. Set a standard for your life, a standard that involves creating a more vital, spiritual life for yourself that in part will affect those around you. Purpose brings meaning to your life. Purpose will help you build, or re-build, your life. And be watchful, for when you least expect it, God will send a runner along side to be there for you.

I encourage you to say NOW! Now is the time to rise, my Sisters of every nation, rise and fly. Spread your wings and test your limits. Watch your dreams lay idle no more, but see, as they will become limitless with God. The Scripture in Isaiah 52:1-2 says:

> "Awake, awake; put on thy strength, O Zion;
> put on thy beautiful garments, O Jerusalem,
> the holy city: for henceforth there shall no
> more come into thee uncircumcised and the unclean.
> Shake thyself from the dust; arise and sit down,
> O Jerusalem: loose thyself from the bands of thy neck,
> O' captive daughter of Zion."

Arise my Sisters, shake off the dust and the noose, put on your strength and go forth. Do not delay! Pursue your dreams, my Sisters, for your silence could cost not only your life, but also the life of someone else.

Chapter 5
A Time To Discover

A flower that blooms in adversity

is a beautiful thing.

- Anonymous

During the journey to discover myself, I stumbled onto how I developed my slave mentality. See, my Sisters, when you are born the life you live brings along restraints, which can mock you, hurt you, kill you, trap you, even victimize you. This mentality helps form and shape your identity while sculpting your life. And in turn you will use it as a measuring stick to help you judge and identify where others stand. This attitude can make or break relationships for you. Until you come into the knowledge that the power of your relationships is what helps you forge and solidify one another, you will continue to fight each other.

My slave mentality developed this way. I did not voice my opinion, my objections or my fears as a child, especially during the period of time when I was being molested. My grandparents had taught me that a good child is seen and not heard. A good child remains quiet until spoken to.

Now, I love history and so my fascination with it did nothing but reinforce my slave mentality. I would watch movies on slavery and instead of being moved by the injustices, I was moved by the fact that the good slaves were quiet and obedient. They did not talk back, but did as they were told. This is how I was. My elders taught me that to talk back was disrespectful, so I never spoke out because I wanted to respect my elders and be a good little girl. However, this mindset carried over into my adulthood. God had to show me how to find my voice and speak out.

When I heard the word *servant*, I would automatically assume it meant *slave*. Webster's dictionary defines them this way.

Servant: one employed to care for someone or his property.

Slave: a person held against his will and made to work for another.

I also began to recognize that with the servant/slave mentality came the eye rolling, teeth sucking, hand on hip motion, and neck popping. This is well known to be associated with women of an ethnic culture. You are taught to do it, so you do it, and it is expected of you to do it. By whom? Society has labeled you as such.

Anyway, as I began my search, I used the Bible to bring more light to the words "servant" and "slave." My research has led to me to this type of definition:

Servant: one who delights in assisting; one
who has a gift to serve, which loves to serve;
one who has the right attitude, the right heart
to give to others just because . . . .

Slave: one who does these things because of force,
guilt, trying to create a giving impression, one who
serves but their hearts are not in it;
one, which does it for show.

Now, which category, my Sisters, do you fall into?

After I did an attitude check, I realized I wanted to have a servant's attitude, not a slave mentality. Once I began to apply this to my life, everything seemed brighter. I did not fool myself though. If I did not want to do it, I would not even volunteer to do it; and if I was asked and unsure, I asked the person to let me think about it and get back with them. There are times, however, when I still slip and end up with the slave mentality. Doing it on remote control and with no heart, but I am learning.

I am no longer a slave, but a woman, a lady. Bishop T. D. Jakes, in his book, *The Lady, Her Lover and Her Lord*, speaks in reference to his mother, which I believe should be the mark of every woman.

He said, "*She was a lady not because of the abundance of wealth she possessed, but the abundance of class she demonstrated.*" We must learn how to serve the King with a servant's attitude and demonstrate class in our serving.

As sisters, it is essential for you to assist one another in each one's efforts to be whole. For if you are immersed in building the Kingdom of God, then you must be concerned with helping your sisters' blossom, fulfilling their potential.

Chapter 6
A Time To Speak

If you can imagine it,

you can create it.

If you can dream it,

you can become it.

- William Arthur Ward

As sisters, sometimes it is hard for you to keep silent, and sometimes it is hard for you to speak. However, when you do find your voice to speak, you speak the same language. This is the language of the heart, of your emotions. You can become strategic players to build confidence, trust, to help through and with defining moments in each ones lives. It is time to kill the pretense that has plagued women for centuries. The one, which says women are two-faced and gossipy, as well as the "b" word.

God did not condemn you to stay away from each other and be lonely. You will need to be lifted up. Understood. Revived. Renewed. Reassured. Loved. Your life does not have to be full of loss, rejection, and abandonment. My Sisters, you can become significant figures of influence in each other's lives, as well as provide security, companionship, and compassion.

Toni McNaron, a noted college professor said, "*A sister can be seen as someone who is both ourselves and very much not ourselves – a special kind of double.*" As sisters, you should strive to be a reflection, not duplication, of the good, which lies within the relationships you develop with other women.

As you gain the confidence of your sisters, you will never cease to be important to each other. In sisterhood, friendships are crucial because you base them on how much you can trust them. My Sisters, you have to offer a fountain or richness and support for one another.

As you develop a relationship of support, you begin to take each other into your confidence, learning each other's secrets, as well as learning how to keep them. The Bible Scripture, "*Do unto others as you would have them do unto you,*" becomes your motto. You should treat others like you want to be treated and should be treated.

So if you are being judgmental, flighty or critical about a sister or anyone, for that matter and then find the same things happening to you, you are reaping what you have sown. If you sow love, grace and mercy, then that is what you will reap. You must look at your life and ask yourself, "What am I sowing?" "What am I reaping?" If you do not like what you see, then set out and change it.

You have been taught not to mind being inconvenienced when one of us calls out for help. The first part of Proverbs 27:10 says, "*Thine own friend, and thy father's friend, forsake not . . .,*" this is the type of bond once forged endures forever, whether you see each other frequently or seldom, whether you are near or far, young or old; for you have found a serendipitous friendship, one of value.

As you pursue your dream, I know you will be happier chasing it and snaring it. I believe this will bring you more joy than burying yourself in the mind games you play, which include "what ifs" and "not being worthy."

When you purpose to spend time in solitude with God, He will restore your soul, your spirit, and your emotions, your whole being. Pursuing your dream, your purpose will also serve as an opportunity to intensify your walk with God and develop within you a resilient spirit.

In the true relationships you will build, it will not require one person to do all the work, but must become a concerted effort. As you bond and grow, will you have conflicts, arguments, and disagreements? Yes, but by the grace of God, and communicating, you can handle it and grow richer in your relationships.

A biblical story of an incredible bonding and love can be found in the story of David and Jonathan in 1st Samuel Chapters 19 and 20, as well as 2nd Samuel Chapter 1. David and Jonathan made a vow to be friends for life, and Jonathan, even as he made the vow knew it to be against the wishes of his father, King Saul. With their lives as examples, it shows you that you are able to be close and committed to each other for life.

As you begin to communicate effectively in the same language, you will develop the ability to talk more openly, honestly and with ease about your love, respect, and joy of God. You are able to thank Him for bringing the gift of relationships in your life. This will allow you to look, at what you want to keep and what you want to throw away, bringing you into being a whole person.

Chapter 7
A Time To Choose

When making your choice in life,

do not neglect to live.

- Samuel Johnson

My Sisters, while trying to free yourself from the tangles of bondage, you must make the right choices along the way. These choices can either free you or further entangle you.

Choice: an act of choosing; an option; the power or chance to choose; an alternative; DISCRIMINATION; judgment.

Choose: pick out; select; decide on a preference.

Decision: the act of making up one's mind; resolution; to decide or settle.

Choice can be a selection, vote, desire, option, wish and preference. *Decision* can be a CHOICE, judgment, conclusion, guess, preference, ruling and decree. Become familiar with these three words because they are necessary in the starting process of fulfilling your dreams.

In this chapter, you will be doing a little exercise concerning your ability to make choices and/or decisions.

HAVE YOU BEEN TAUGHT TO MAKE DECISIONS?

Some of the education you may have receive during your school years have not taught you how to properly evaluate circumstances, look at or consider a situation before making a choice or decision. Even sadder is the fact some households or families do not teach or encourage their children to make decisions.

The choices and decisions you have made (*past*), you make (*present*), or will have to make (*future*) will have an EFFECT on your life and those around you which may be involved in the decision-making process. Your choices or decisions, whether good or bad, have repercussions, good and bad.

How would you say your ability is in helping you to make

accurate and just decisions? Do you make decisions quickly? Slowly? With all the facts? When it comes to drugs, do you think you would make the right choice? Stealing? Sex? Peer pressure?

Are these decisions any easier to make when compared to picking out what to wear or what to eat? Do you weigh or compare your choices? How many of you would consider, or have considered, the consequences of some choices you have made or have to make? If you do not remember anything else which you have read in this book, commit this to your memory: **CHOICES FORM and SHAPE YOUR LIFE!**

Think about the choices you have made which have placed you where you are right now. Now, what about the choices you need to make in order to change your life? So, where do you turn to help you make your choices? Before you start to yell "JESUS," you better consider the words of your mouth, for they will either put you in covenant with God, or they will take you out of covenant with Him. It is so easy to say "Jesus," but do you really mean it when you say it?

The Scriptures state if you choose Jesus, He will help you make the RIGHT decisions, those, which are just. Proverbs 3:4-6 says,

"So shall thou find favour and good understanding
in the sight of God and man. Trust in the Lord with
all thine heart; and lean not unto thine own understanding.
In all thy ways acknowledge him, and he shall direct thy paths."

You are admonished to trust God and acknowledge Him, so that you may have favor with God and man. Yeah, sometimes you will miss it and screw up, but that does not mean you will not have to put forth the effort to trust in God anymore or in yourself. Like in Matthew 6:33, if you seek the Kingdom of God first, He will guide you to making the right choices.

Here is a little exercise for you to try. First, I want you to write out three BIG decisions you need to make I mean really big! Not what you are going to eat or wear, but something major like, what college do you want to attend? What do you want to major in? Do you have a desire to start your own business? What it would be? What career do you want to pursue? Is it time to move and buy a house, or a new car? Should I marry this person or not?

What I consider to be BIG is: *"God, what is YOUR PLAN for my life?"* You are aware that He has plans for you, and if you do not get with the program now, you might not get with it later.

Second, find a Scripture or inspirational/motivational quote, which matches the decision you are focusing on. The instructions you want so badly are found in the Word of God, in the Bible. By quoting the Scripture and doing this research for your plan, you are not focusing on your problems 24/7, but taking an active role in by getting involved in your life.

Third, begin to pray about the choice and/or decision. How will you know if it is right? You will know because you will have a different peace, a calm that you did not have before you began this process. I encourage you to continue to press in and tear down those walls, so you can build on a firmer foundation.

When I began to really focus on this book, I had to encourage myself with a Scripture. I would find myself quoting Jeremiah 29:11 *"For I know the thoughts that I think toward you, saith the Lord, thoughts of peace, and not of evil, to give you an expected end."* It was the "expected" end that kept my attention and which in turn, kept me focused on the task at hand. Finding a Scripture to stand on will help keep you grounded.

My Soul Desire

My soul desire is to be a vessel, which brings life,
Life, in the midst of all the anger,
bitterness, unforgiveness, and strife.
My soul desire is to help others live in harmony,
Hand in hand,
So all can see,
God inside of you and me.

Though storms may come,
They will also cease,
Though strong winds will blow,
They, too, will be followed by peace,
Though things go wrong,
As often they will,
My soul desire is to see you learn to stand still,
And see you fulfill God's will.

Yes, there will be times that you will bend,
Yes, there will be times when you will weep,
Yes, there will be times when all will seem to be lost,
But, if you stand still,
Then you will see,
The hand of God moving, for you and me.

My soul desire is to see,
You standing strong, firm, and planted,
Free from bondage,
Deeply rooted like a tree.

- *Java L. Collins*

"But we have this treasure

in earthen vessels,

that the excellency of the power

may be of God, and not of us.

We are troubled on every side,

yet not distressed;

we are perplexed,

but not in despair;

Persecuted, but not

forsaken; cast down,

but not destroyed."

- 2 Corinthians 4:79

part II

A Time to Gain Strength
A Time to Heal
A Time for Challenges
A Time to Be Awakened
A Time to Laugh
A Time to Love
A Time to Embrace
A Woman Unfinished

Chapter 8
A Time To Gain Strength

Trust in yourself.

Your perceptions are often

more accurate than you

are willing to believe.

- Claudia Blake

SUDDENLY! A hand reaches out and snatches me up before it is too late, before I fall and hit the bottom. I begin to feel the warmth as I slowly roll away from the murky, mirth of the grave that is beginning to encompass me. I squint as I see the light. I feel something, which is so strange, so new, resurging in me. I feel love once more.

Unknowingly from where it comes, it washes over me like a ray of sunshine, bringing with it life. Old dreams are renewed, rebirthed from deep within me, and once again. I am no longer bound by having my circumstances rule me, but me ruling over my circumstances.

A voice, which is so soft and gentle, urges me to rise up and take my place, a place that has been ordained for me since the beginning of time. Rise up and take my rightful place in life! Sure, I have been battered and bruised. Sure, I have lost some of those battles. Sure, I have been wounded, and some of my sisters have been wounded and left for dead, but RISE UP!

****

You have been through some hard times, some very hard times; I do not deny what the past will say about you, but it is time to RISE UP! If you look close, real close, you will find something deep inside of you. Something that you never even noticed was there before. No, you never even noticed it while you were weeping and wailing.

You never even noticed it while going about your daily tasks. You never even noticed it while at a stand still in life. Even when you were falling, it was there all along. You never even noticed the STRENGTH you had gained. You never even noticed your resilience to keep on when others had given up.

Finally, you realized that you could NOT do it on your own. It is time to hang up your superwoman cape and stop being everything to everybody. It just does not work anymore. You never even realized that this "inner strength" is what has kept you going all this time. See, my Sisters, this is that "suddenness" in your life, which makes things happen miraculously and quickly.

Larnell Harris sings a song titled, *I Can Begin Again,* and in it he has a line that says "*and new beginnings are not just for the young.*" Do not think because you are older you can no longer go after a dream, or have that dream revived. Age is just a number. I want to see your dream fulfilled; but more so, I want you to see your dream fulfilled. But in order to do that, you have to start dreaming again.

I am not talking foolish dreams, those that help you to "*escape reality temporarily*" dreams. I am talking about the dream, which you were obsessed with as a child and buried it so deep within you, that to whisper about it makes you gasp. The dream you wanted to do so badly, you could taste it. See, this dream is the one that made you ache inside, like you would just die, if it did not come forth. Your eyes would tear up and joy would fill your heart, just to think about it. Go back in time to when you first fell in love, and how that feeling of love made you feel good all over, this is the dream I am talking about.

This dream, which was dashed or shattered, especially when the person you loved the most, denied it, laughed at it, scoffed at it. They even thought of it as being foolish. That person never tried to help you realize the potential lurking deep within you, just waiting to get out. The dream, which you loved with all your heart, had it manifested; you would have given your very life for it.

An example of this would be as a child I dreamed of becoming a ballet dancer. I went so far as to research the basic steps of ballet and taught them to myself. When practicing one day in my room my dream was shattered by words from a grandmother who stated, "*You will never be a ballet dancer.*" Later in life I picked up dance again by teaching others from my own personal love of my dream of becoming a ballet dancer. A dream restored and fulfilled.

When your opponents voiced loudly and softly that it was impossible to accomplish, you buried it deeper still within. As your own mind spoke doubts and fears, it crashed against the rocks during the storm and sunk to the bottom, waiting for such a time as this. Waiting to be resurrected. Waiting for you to give your life for its worth.

That, my Sisters, is the dream we are going for. THAT dream which is locked deep inside of you. THAT dream which is a part of you just like your hair, your hands, your feet. THIS is the dream that I desire to help you bring out. THIS dream is a reflection of your for it is you! Birthed out of your spirit. THIS dream will stand the test of time. THIS dream is the dream, my Sisters, that I believe with all my heart, my spirit, my soul and my body that God wants you to have, to breathe life into, to bring forth to live!

Les Brown says in his book, *Live Your Dream*, "*That is why it is so important for you to hold on to a vision of who you want to be and where you want to go. It is equally important to fashion a vision of what you want to leave behind.*" I encourage you, my Sisters; as you change yourself, strive to leave a legacy, one built with the warmth of your love, tenacity, and integrity.

Chapter 9
A Time To Heal

Where it was dark,

now there's light.

Where there was pain,

now there's joy.

Where there was weakness,

I found my strength.

- Celine Dion, New Day

To God, you are accepted, important, special and loved. To Him, you are His life. He has His Being tied up in you; you are made in His likeness, His image. The Bible declares this in Psalms 139:14,

> *"I will praise thee; for I am fearfully and wonderfully made: marvellous are thy work; and that my soul knoweth right well."*

In this psalm, David is acknowledging that he is made very well because God is the craftsman, and God does not do shabby work. I want to see you realize that the One who made you did not do a shabby job. It is my desire to see my Sisters, as well as myself, loose and free. It is my belief that you nor I desire to stay in bondage.

There is a longing, almost a sense of urgency, to move on and become free in the process. To become freer than you have ever been. To be able to look back at where you have been, laugh and rejoice freely concerning where you are going.

I desire to see you become women of excellence, love, grace and mercy. However, in order to achieve this, it requires something of you. It requires you to let go of others. No, it doesn't mean you stop caring. It does mean that you stop trying to live your life through other people.

There is a desire among women to have the noose loosened. You know, the invisible rope, which seems to have you by the throat. The one that seems to have you bound, strung up by your feet, with your hands constrained, your mouth gagged and your mind closed. It is time to be free, to remove the noose, the rope from your entire being.

Yes, there will be a time when you are able to look at the wounds and scars, and yet, know that though you have been through a battle, you were still left standing, and alive. To know that it was the strength, which God put in you, which has allowed you to succeed.

To know that God is in the process of healing you — spiritually, physically, emotionally, mentally — healing your "WHOLE" person, so that you can become a "HOLY" person. Yes, my Sisters, you are more than able to possess this land, this temple, and this body, because God says you are entitled to have and live your dreams.

You become restored in dignity, selfesteem, integrity, and love. You know and become aware of what you were, while learning who you are, and yearning to see yourself as God sees you. This is what you must strive towards. You must realize that the rejection you faced had nothing to do with you, but with who you are destined to be and who you are called to serve, an awesome God!

God is speaking to your broken, mutilated, wounded spirit and body. He is calling you

His lace, His silk, His satin, His sunrise and sunset, His hope, His love, His dreams and visions, His fragrance. He is calling to the beauty in you that you have never seen before, touched, or even caught a glimpse of in yourself. He is calling your name, my Sisters. Now, I say to you:

Rise up, my Sisters,
rise, be made whole, rejoice
and be on your way to:

H = HEALTH
E = ENDURANCE
A = ATTITUDE
L = LIFE, LOVE
I = INTERGRITY
N = NEWNESS
G = GOD

HEALING!"

Please do not come to the end of your life, full of sorrows, regrets, or blame. For everywhere you turn, may you come out "in God." You do not have to let the "stuff" get you down. Learn to monitor your response to those things that push your buttons.

It is time, as Pastor Émil Hawkins says, to get rid of the *"stinking thinking,"* those thoughts or ways of thinking which keep you bound, gagged, confused. You now have a choice to make. Will it be bondage or freedom? Which one will you choose, my Sister?

Though times get hard and all seems lost, I pray that you will choose to arise, for you are a daughter of Zion! By making yourself vulnerable, you make yourself stronger.

Leo Buscaglia stated in his video, *The Art of Being Fully Human*: *"You can't celebrate anyone in the world until you celebrate yourself."*

I believe that during your healing process, you need to celebrate who you are in Christ, who He created you to be. You need to celebrate yourself. Begin to unlock your spirit, unlock your soul, and learn to stop being afraid of letting go of positions and running other people's lives. You will not disappoint them. The only one being let down and getting disappointed is you. You take the time to commend and celebrate others; when will you take the time to celebrate you? When will you take the time to recognize that you are free?

You are free! You no longer have to be someone else, or continue to let others lock you into their mold. You are free! I learned a valuable lesson during the time I was writing this book. I learned I had let other people, who had good intentions, lock me into being who they THOUGHT I should be. Then one night while crying out to God, He spoke to me:

"Don't let anyone change you.
I created you to have a gentle

spirit, because if everyone had
a warring spirit, where would
the balance be? I love you for
who you are, not because
you are trying to be someone else.
Relax. Enjoy yourself, as you begin
to DISCOVER WHO YOU ARE."

So, I say to you, my Sisters:

> *Rise up, celebrate life, and enjoy yourself as*
> *you discover who you are — spirit, mind, and body.*

It is time to fight for what is rightfully yours, for what you are entitled to!

.

Chapter 10
A Time For Challenges

A gem cannot be polished

without friction,

nor can we be perfected

without trial.

- Our Daily Bread, September 2003

Do the thing you are afraid to do and the death of fear is certain.

- Ralph Waldo Emerson

I heard it said once that *people who do not know the value of their gifts, their dreams, their visions, are easy prey*. The challenge: finding someone who will remind you of the preciousness of your gift, your dream. So are you ready to begin? Are you ready to accept the challenge and act on it? Are you ready to fortify yourself to where you do not become easy prey?

There are only two things, which I can think of at this very minute that would make you want to say no. One is that your past is holding your in bondage; and two is you are waiting on circumstances and situations to line up with how you think they should be before getting started. By waiting on things to get right, I am talking about things such as raising your children, getting the right mate, losing weight, getting the right job, etc. You let these things keep you from pursuing your dreams and desires. However, the challenge that your past presents may prove to be the most difficult.

Your past can be your enemy. And some of those people, circumstances, situations that are linked to your past, would prefer that things stay just the way they are. Even, if it means that you continue to feel unhappy, hopeless, wallowing in despair. You know the old saying "misery loves company." There will even be some people in your present, and even in your future, who will not want you to succeed, but as you gain ground and confidence, you will be able to stand up to them. I pray that at this point in reading this book you have now decided **not** to be miserable anymore. You have decided, enough is enough, and you have had **ENOUGH!** Isaiah 43:18-19 says:

> *"Remember ye not the former things,*
> *neither consider the things of old.*
> *Behold, I will do a new thing;*
> *now it shall spring forth; shall you not*
> *know it? I will even make a way in the*
> *wilderness, and rivers in the desert."*

You have made a choice, and God has said I am going to do a new thing for you because of your choice. God will tell you when you think all is lost that He becomes the ultimate Way-maker. He is going to give you a plan to bring you out. Joyce Meyer once ministered that *"separation from things of the past is one of the prices you pay for progress."* You must pay a price for your dream to evolve. Even the Word, the Holy Bible, tells you that God has a plan for you to prosper, but it says nothing about it being tied to your past.

God has created you as a unique, original miracle. There is not another you in this whole vast universe. Though you have your parents' DNA, you are not a copy of them, your grandparents or of someone else. Yes, you have some of your parents and grandparents' traits, but you are not them.

Some time ago, Pastor Émil Hawkins did a message concerning the principles of relationships. He was speaking on how relationships are supposed to be beneficial to both parties. Then he spoke a statement so profound, that it reverberated in my being, in my very spirit:

"If I am not free in my spirit, then I will always be somebody's slave or a slave to something."

As you begin again, ask yourself, *"What or who am I a slave to?"* Do not be afraid to recognize it! If you are a slave to the television, say so. If you cannot go one day without watching the "Young and the Restless" say so. Then realize, you were not struck dead because you were honest with yourself. However, God will challenge you to make a change.

My personal experience has taught me that the "Why me? Syndrome" prolongs where I am. I have learned to say to others, and myself "I have got to be me." Me! Me! Not the "me" who my friends are comfortable with, but the "me" I am learning to be comfortable with.

People, as well as the enemy, get nervous when you begin to announce who you are. They get really nervous when you start to pursue that dream. Why? One reason is because they begin to feel left out, rejected, like they have been kicked to the curb! They feel that you do not need them anymore.

Anyone who does not celebrate you, but tolerates you, is not a friend; and it is time to let him or her go and hook up with someone who *can* celebrate the "real" you. Look at those around you. Identify who is for you and who is against you.

I am learning I need to build *"safe"* relationships to help me get by and stay in pursuit of my dream. What I mean when I say safe relationships is that I am learning to surround myself with people who have my "best interest" at heart.

These are the ones who will be honest with me and still love me. They have seen my flaws, know that I have them, and will not attack me because of them. They accept flaws, all of me. I do not have to pretend when I am with them. I can be honest and open while receiving their love and their support.

Your relationships will become like 2 Corinthians 2:7-8: "*So that contrariwise ye ought rather to forgive him, and comfort him, lest perhaps such a one should be swallowed up with overmuch sorrow. Wherefore, I beseech you that ye would confirm your love toward him.*" If you make a mistake, you must acknowledge it and continue in the love of Christ. You do not ignore or avoid each other because of mistakes that have been made. You work together to bring teaching and understanding of what happened and why.

Like your past, time will try to rob you as well. I once heard that there are four attitudes of time:

1) Wasted time: buried opportunities;

2) Marked time: the meter is running regardless of what you do;

3) Redeemed time: making up for lost time; and

4) Transcended time: somewhere in the future.

Find out where you are, and then decide where you would like to be.

Yes, there will be times, which you will hurt and you will begin to wonder if the pain will ever end and if you have made the right decisions. I, too, have been there. Sometimes you have to get hit many times before you finally wake up and take control of your life again.

And then, you are able to realize that with the breaking of each new day, with the sun rising, the pain lessens, and you can breathe a little more freer, move a little less restricted, and see a little more clearly, for the Lord, your God, is with you. He is there by way of the Holy Spirit, to help, instruct, guide, and comfort when necessary. He is there to strengthen you and help manifest your dreams through different stages until they become something physical, something more than a thought or vision, something . . . REAL!

So, are you ready to take the risk and begin? You need to begin to gain confidence in who you are and be who God has called you to be. There is power when a dream is fulfilled.

Chapter 11
A Time To Be
Awakened

*The most terrifying thing is
to accept oneself completely.*

- Carl Jung

The awakening to pursue your dream is a process. The steps outlined here are key parts to this process. To start, this calls for you to be honest with yourself.

First, recognize where you are.

Second, begin to search inside for that dream which is lying hidden, dormant, waiting to be discovered. List your assets.

Third, begin to seek for a person or two, in whom you can confide. This person must be someone you can trust. If you do not, then pray and ask God to send you someone to confide in, keeping in mind it may be God Himself who wants you to confide in Him. Prayer is communicating with God – talking and listening.

You want to develop a symbiotic relationship with God and those who you believe are sent to help you. This simply means you want to develop an intimate (non-sexual) relationship that says though we are different; this relationship can be mutually beneficial to all involved.

The point of this relationship is to provide a balance in order to pursue your dream. Godly, sisterly love will provide a balance for you in your relationships as you pursue your dream. Having someone as a sounding board, counselor, or friend, is an important aspect in your pursuit. I cannot stress it enough, you want someone just as committed as you are to your dreams, to your success. Also, recognize an important part of the relationship is growing up together – learning how to fight, how to forgive, and how to work things out in love.

Fourth, write down on paper what you want to change initially. Habakkuk 2:2 tell you to write the vision and make it plain, for it has an appointed or set time to make its appearance. Do not make it so big that you will back down at the first sign of not seeing a change. Do not live or drift off into a fantasy, a world of unreality. Open your eyes and prepare the plan to pursue your dream. What

I am saying is do not put down something you wish, but something you believe in. In writing or developing your plan, be detailed in your steps toward achieving your dream.

Fifth, honor your actions on what you value most. This will make you genuine, reliable, trusting and help with your self-discipline.

Sixth, learn to cultivate respect of yourself. This will help develop and promote inner security and commitment to your dream. Give it everything you have.

Seventh, recognize your specific skill set and the aptitude that you have. Every person has a given set of specific disposition, which she does well. Recognize them and use them.

Eighth, remember not to beat yourself up, in your mind or verbally, if you mess up. Everyone makes mistakes. So just start over and try again! Do not get discouraged. Become encouraged!

Ninth, pick out a scripture or saying that is encouraging to you. Place it in your bedroom, bathroom, and/or kitchen. Put it somewhere you can see it to serve as a reminder of your journey.

Finally, if you must use your past, then use it as a key of knowledge and experience for your present and use it to help propel you into your future. Find a mirror and allow yourself to look into it. Look past the outer surface to the beauty, and see what God sees within you. I remember the first time I did this; I thought this was so stupid. However, when I did it, determined to see with God's eyes, then I saw a woman of God, the apple of His eye. Someone He trusted enough to place a dream inside a vessel to be carried and birthed at an appointed time. For truly change is . . . a journey.

The key to survival is to make yourself vulnerable; for within your vulnerability you find and gain strength. If you do not find within yourself the courage to leave or begin again, and move on, then death and destruction awaits. This choice will eventually have the final say.

Is this what you want to be your key . . . death? Do you want to keep your spirit and your dream buried, locked up? Or do you want to live, and love the life you are living? I guess this is why 2 Corinthians 4:8-9 is one of my favorite Scriptures: "*We are troubled on every side, yet not distressed; we are perplexed, but not in despair; Persecuted, but not forsaken; cast down, but not destroyed!*"

There will be times when the going gets tough, but I shall rise again, because of Whose I am and Who is in me. But I also realize I have to make the choice to rise up, and not lay wallowing in the mud! So, I may be down for a while, but I will never be out of the game of life. I shall always choose to rise!

And this is my challenge to you as you pursue that dream which has been awakened inside of you. When it looks like the mountain is unclimbable, or the way looks impassable, press on anyhow, for you are close to becoming victorious in yet another area in your life, and are able to go on to the next level in the pursuit of your dream.

I read a book titled *What Looks Like Crazy On An Ordinary Day* by Pearl Cleage, and there was a phrase that just stuck with me. It went like this, "*Sometimes you meet yourself on the road before you have a chance to learn the appropriate greeting. Faced with your own possibilities, the hard part is knowing a speech is not required. All you have to say is yes.*"

My Sisters, I say to you in order to choose how you want to be, just say yes. All you have to do to live again my Sisters is say **yes**. And know this, sometimes, the journey will get a little tough, a little hard, and it is okay to sit down for a moment. I was watching a beautiful sunset and heard these words:

Sometimes the best things in life are free,
Meadows, the sun, flowers, and fun.

Sometimes the best things in life are free,
Running, laughing, cheering, crying.
Sometimes the best things in life are free,
Giving, sharing, the kiss of someone.
Sometimes the best things in life are free,
Like Jesus, God's Son, gave His life for everyone.
Sometimes the best things in life are free,
My purpose, my dreams, my being.

Find a sunrise or sunset, and re-read these words. Let them inspire you, motivate you, move you to action, and create peace inside of you. And remember, you do not have to understand everything about your dream in order to get started. Now, get up and go!

Chapter 12
A Time To Laugh

We have to laugh.

Because laughter,

we already know,

is the first evidence

of freedom.

- Rosario Castellanos

Learning to laugh again was the hardest, yet the most liberating thing I have ever done. Laughter freed my soul and in the process began to unlock the potential that was lying dormant inside of me. It gave me the liberty to love myself, unashamedly, and regardless of what others thought, said, or their actions or lack thereof, and brought me back to a freedom that I could not have attained elsewhere. No one or no thing could have given it to me.

When laughter returned to my house, it brought with it freshness, which had long ago been absent. It brought a joy so exhilarating that I did not want to stop laughing. I held it close, while guarding it well, for I have no wish for it to leave. When I get down, I remember the laughter and how it came, and then suddenly I feel like a burst of sunshine is getting ready to cut loose from my body as the laughter starts to bubble up.

I believe now more than ever that laughter is a precious commodity, which few of us partake of fully. We do a surface laughter the majority of the time, but the laughter I am speaking of resonates from deep within, and explodes like a volcano after being pent up for so long. It is a hearty laughter, one, which at times can bring tears to your eyes, warmth to your soul, and color to your cheeks.

I realized I had stopped laughing when my mother died on June 12, 1991. My surface laughter became part of my mask, which in turn had become part of myself. Laughter reminded me of the joy, the friendship, and love I felt when I had spent time with my mother. So I distanced myself from anything that reminded me of those good times because it hurt to know she was not with me any longer.

This went on for about eight years. During the final year of earning my Masters in Human Relations, I was taking a course taught by Dr. Katherine Jones at the University of Oklahoma. Though the course dealt with education, in it we studied the effects of laughter. As we began to study, I began to wonder if ever I would laugh again.

At the same time, I was also attending a Christian workshop called Breath of Life, and realized the reason why I did not laugh was because I did not want to remember my mother's death and not being able to see her before she died. I had not dealt with the grief phase because I was too busy putting everyone else's needs before my own. So, I did what was only natural and expected of me – I buried it.

As I started to deal with the grief of losing my mother, I began to heal, not just physically, but spiritually, emotionally, and mentally. I began to address issues in my life that I no longer wanted to be hindrances to me. I knew that healing really began to take place on May 14, 1999, the night my son graduated from high school.

I was always apprehensive and wanted my family to accept me for who I was and not who they think I should have been. Then the most wonderful thing happened – I started to laugh again, for I realized I had to first learn to accept myself for who I was before expecting anybody else to.

This was a wonderful change, a necessary one in order for me to begin to live again and love again. A beautiful laughter, which even now still rings in my ears. A healthy laugh, not a surface one. A joyful laugh and not one full of sorrow. I realized fully for the first time I am a truly loved individual and that I really do have something worthwhile to give. It may not be a martyr style giving, but it will impart into the lives of those whom I touch.

I was finally beginning to feel free to be me, to heal, to laugh, to love, but most of all to live. I finally have the strength to pursue my purpose, my passion, my life's calling without hindrance. I finally am able to accept myself, which is the most important thing of all.

My Sisters, you must learn to accept and love yourself, even if no one else does. You spend so much time looking for affirmation from others, from accomplishments, from goals set, when all you have to do is to search and look deep within of yourself. You need to learn to guard yourself against the words of other people. For these words will cling to your mind and get deeply rooted into your soul, and serve as stumbling blocks to achieving your dream.

You need to learn to say, *"That's how they feel, but I choose not to let it rule me. What they say is not a reflection of who I am, or my feelings. So I choose not to let their words affect me."*

If they are offering wisdom or advice, do the following:

1) hear it,
2) weigh it out (meaning does it relate to you, your situation, etc.),
3) pray about it, and
4) make a choice, whether to accept, shelve it or reject it.

I received an important revelation during this process, I learned that I placed others opinions of me over what I thought of myself. Regardless of whether their words portrayed good or bad, positive or negative, whatever they spoke I became. I began to recognize I had low self-esteem because I had allowed the words of others to mold me.

Learn to guard yourself, because everyone who comes into your life is not coming to make a deposit, but at times to make a withdrawal, and these withdrawals have a negative impact. Remember, my Sisters, life is not only a journey, but also a process, a never-ending time to learn, to grow, to mature.

Les Brown writes in his book, *Live Your Dreams*, the following statement:

> *"You have to know what is right for you and go after it regardless of what others say. Others judge you based on what they have seen you do. You must operate on the basis*

of your vision for yourself. Nobody is going to care more about your goals than you. Nobody is going to put more time in on them than you. You have to find your own source of hunger and motivation and let it drive you."

My source of hunger and motivation stemmed from pleasing God and being happy with what I chose to do. When I am in my dream, my element, I flow. I am focused and committed to fulfilling what I have placed before me. It is an experience that I cannot accurately describe. It brings me joy, peace, calmness and pleasure all at the same time.

My Sisters, I encourage you to find the right fit for you. Push what others have to say out of your mind, because they will judge everything you do based on what they have seen previously. Now, there are handfuls that will encourage and get behind you to keep you going. Those are the ones you want in your corner during this process. And when you begin this process, do it ONE STEP at a time.

You will begin to tap into your potential, your dream, and your vision. There will be times that you will have to dig deep and pull to call up your purpose, your deepest dream. Know that it will take time.

My dear friend, Georgia told me one day she saw me as a big bird locked up in a cage that was too little for me. She said she watched as the bird struggled to be free and thought if that bird does not get free soon, she will die. I soon began to realize life was locked up in me struggling to be free, not wanting to die, but to live.

So I write to you, my Sisters, stop struggling to be free, and let go and be free! Breathe again! Love again! But most of all learn to live and laugh again!

Chapter 13
A Time To Love

For all this I considered

in my heart

even to declare all this,

that the righteous, and the wise,

and their works,

are in the hand of God:

no man knoweth

either love or hatred

by all that is before them.

- Ecclesiastes 9:1

The writer of Ecclesiastes is basically telling us that the dead know nothing. They have taken secrets with them to the grave that will never be told by them. Alexander Smith said that *"love is the discovery of ourselves in others and the delight put in the recognition."* Intimacy can be defined as the ultimate confines of one's capacity to love. Intimacy requires trust. It is not done out of neediness or dependency. You must learn not to be overwhelmed by a person's vulnerability, or by the revelation of their private faults.

Revealing yourself means placing yourself in the limelight for critical, sometimes harsh, judgments, whether positive or negative. Value, comfort, and pleasure should come with intimacy. Love and intimacy should be wholesome. A healthy self-esteem and self-acceptance will give you the courage to take risks and reap rewards.

I had to find and am finding the courage to risk in order to gain. Learning to trust myself, set boundaries and develop deep, intimate friendships was something I had to open up and learn to do. When my expectations are not met, I am learning that I will not keel over and die. Now realizing that when love is free, healthy, and genuine, that it is impossible to love too much. I do not need a man to complete me or validate me. I am developing respect and value for myself.

The desire for love is a fundamental human drive. No matter who you are or what you do, whether you are male or female, married or single, you want the exact same thing when it comes to love. Someone to enjoy life's experiences with, someone to make you laugh, someone who understands your fears and sorrows, and someone who loves you and knows how to make you feel good about yourself.

There is one basic underlying reason why most of us find love so difficult to achieve. And basically that is we have no idea what love really is, what to look for, and can only identify with what we have been exposed to. And usually this is not based on the Word of God.

You begin your search for love not only with sincere and realistic goals, but also with primitive deep-rooted fantasies. The fairy tales and myths, which you hear from the crib and expect to manifest in the natural when you reach adulthood; only to find yourself disillusioned and disappointed when the knight in shining armor does not appear to whisk you away. You must come to realize that you do not live in the fairy tale world, but the real one.

Learn to love and value yourself. I heard it said that each of us has our own thorns. The thorns can be many things – being overweight, financially distraught, children, low self-esteem, marital difficulties, etc. In all fairness, when you compare yourself to others, you place yourself at a disadvantage, because you do not know what the other person has gone through to get where she is nor does she know what you have had to go through to get where you are!

The facts of life are there will always be someone prettier, smarter, with a bigger house and a fancier car. There will always be someone whose children will do better, and have husbands who will be better. Learn to grow where you are planted, and let go of the things that are robbing you of your value. When you compare yourself to other sisters, you rob yourself and them of your true value, and this interferes with the manifestation of your dream.

These unconscious forces are what shape your need to love and be loved. The quest for love is motivated by three powerful unconscious wishes:

1) the desire for fusion (your wish for completion),

2) validation (your need to feel good about yourself), and

3) aliveness (your desire to be excited about life, the pursuit of romance, intense emotions).

My Sisters, I implore you to begin to explore what you want out of this life, right now. The key is that by loving yourself, you open up the doors of possibility for others to love you as well. Whether you are a mother, grandmother, aunt, single, married, divorced, I want to encourage you to take advantage of this opportunity and make the choice now.

A late civil rights leader by the name of Whitney Young, Jr., said, "*It is better to be prepared for an opportunity and not have one than to have an opportunity and not be prepared.*" Use this time wisely to prepare yourself for the entrance into the next leg of your journey. A journey in which you hold the reins to your destiny.

Ephesians 6:10 says, "*Finally, my brethren, be strong in the Lord, and the power of His might.*" Be encouraged, remain strong and be who God has created you to be. Look at this opportunity as a chance to grow. It is time for you to stop doing activities that are not producing positive outcomes in your life, but strive for opportunities to produce or bring forth change in your life.

Remember: "*You are somebody and you have something to give.*" Someone, somewhere is waiting for you to be set free. You hold the key to someone else's freedom in the palm of your hand. So get prepared to dream a little dream, but live a larger life to fulfill not only you, but to impact others.

Mother Teresa once said "*Intense love does not measure, it just gives.*" Your impact on others is done in love and it will not measure to your expected return. An example of intense love is God giving His Son for us. He does not measure how much He gets in return, but whether we will accept His offer of unconditional love. My Sisters, accept His offer now of unconditional love. Use it to pursue your dream and impact those in your path.

Chapter 14
A Time To Embrace

Only by embracing change

can we mold it

in a way that benefits all of us.

- Lewis Jaffe, Fast Company, June 2000

My Sisters, know this, once you make the choice to pursue, to find your dream, you will be adding to your worth. You are valuable to God, and I believe when you step into what God has called you to do, you will add to your worth, your value in the Kingdom of God. Your dream adds to your value. Are you embracing your worth?

As I stated earlier, my purpose is to stir, to inspire women to revisit their dreams, pick them up, blow the dust off of them % look at them and see the untapped jewel which God has given them – then toss out the excuses and run with the dream, the vision, bringing it to full manifestation. To search for and regain its value or worth that was put down in pursuit of other things.

I sense your dreams are God's way of calling you back to your first love – Him. He begins by bringing the desire back to you and stirring it up from smoldering embers to a flame. Stirring it to the point that you must do something about it, and as Dr. Myles Munroe so eloquently put it: *We now have to go to the manufacturer*, the Creator to retrieve an answer. The pursuit of your dreams places you in a position to search God out for fulfillment.

Now, when I speak of dreams, I am not speaking about those crazy dreams brought about by something you ate, but a dream, a vision, a purpose that you know that God has placed in your heart, that He alone has shown you – a passion or love for something that you desire to do which is so deep and so profound, to think about it takes your breath away, and it is something you know you cannot achieve on your own.

Webster defines dream as *"a series of mental images, ideas and emotions occurring in certain stages of sleep; to have ambition, to consider something feasible."* When you have a dream to be birthed by God, you have AMBITION! You have something that is considered feasible, achievable. Hallelujah!

If you are married, this message is not saying leave your husband to pursue your dream, but begin to trust God to make a way for your dream to come to pass. I am here to get you excited about the deposit that God has made in your spirit. Your dream is something, which God has entrusted to your care for such a time as this. Even this alone is something to get excited about. Hallelujah!! That God would entrust something this precious to your care until the time of its manifestation.

When you dare to pursue your dreams, my Sisters, you must prepare yourself to assess the roads that lie before you. Which one will you take? You must be prepared to enter a time of transition, where nothing will seem stable. Where you will speak and cry out to the Lord, yet, hear nothing but stillness. I believe when you decide to pursue your dreams, your gifts, your talents are keys to having your dreams manifest.

The Proverbs 31 woman is an example of this. She dreamed of being a total woman in Christ and it manifested to the point where people would only sing her praises, for her virtues outweighed her faults. When you pursue God with all that is within you, your virtues will far outweigh your faults. I encourage you to no longer let what you do, stop or keep you from being who you are called to be in Christ!

When life happens, please do not quit! But fortify yourself up in your faith, put on your armor, and pursue the choice you have made to have your dream manifest. Stop comparing yourself to others. As women, you develop what Pastor Darrell Hines calls "*comparisionitis.*" You compare yourself to where other sisters are, where you should be in life, regardless of what roads taken and you always come up short.

Contrary to popular belief, the grass is NOT always greener on the other side, and if it is, you can bet there is a higher cost to it! Are you willing to pay the cost to have someone else's life, especially when you do not know what it is? Christ paid the cost for you to live a life that is pleasing and acceptable to Him, which if you were to really look at it, that life would be pleasing to you as well. You cannot have what somebody else has if you are not willing to go through what they went through.

You need to know God wants good things to happen for you, and they are supposed to happen to you because you are an heir to the Kingdom! Often you have allowed preferences of others to force you into a role, which makes you uncomfortable. You do what they say to keep them from being mad at you. You begin to deny yourself your right to proceed with your dreams, your goals, and your God-given promises.

And now I say, to you my Sisters, no more! Push until something happens! I am trying to earnestly convey to those who are unmotivated that in them lies the potential to succeed. Though problems persist, opportunities for your dreams, your passions will come. Do not be afraid to make mistakes. We all make them; none of us are perfect!

Your dreams, your passions are part of what makes you a unique woman of God. Do not allow the world or someone else's preferences to define your dream. Know your call in God's plan, dream it, receive it, and obey it! When you begin to dream again, your value will be restored, or in some cases, increased. Jesus sees through your despair, your sin and restores your worth. I heard it said numerous occasions that time is a privilege; however, spending it wisely is your responsibility. Learn to enjoy the opportunities that God has set before you, and go after the dreams the Father has willed to you.

Be like the daughters of Zelophehad, in Numbers 27. Their father did not have a son, so the council did not want to give them land because their father had died before the Israelites entered the promise land. The daughters got together, went to Moses and basically said:

Yes, we are women, but we are blessed women, and we have a right to walk as others who are blessed!' And they were given their father's possession! They got an inheritance! Hallelujah! God cares for you and desires the best for you. He wants you to have your inheritance; it is the enemy who does not want you to take possession of it. Note the Scripture from I Chronicles 22:19a, it says:

> "Now set your heart and your soul
> to seek the Lord your God . . ."

My Sisters, I want to encourage us to set your heart and soul to seek God.

Chapter 15
A Woman Unfinished

"Change can be exhilarating,

joyous, liberating.

But it can also be terrifying . . .

you are questioning

your very identity

and sense of value.

But take the risk.

It's worth it."

- Dee Hock, Fast Company, July/August 1999

As an accomplished professional with more than twenty plus years of progressive responsibility, I realized I desired to contribute more to life than what I had been. My previous experiences ranged from being an Intelligence Analyst in the United States Army to an Executive Administrative Assistant to presidents and CEOs to being an elementary educator. In all of my positions, I had been given the opportunity to teach and/or train, and had done so with enthusiasm and flair. Though these experiences were enjoyable, invaluable, and challenging, they still left me lacking.

Robert Frost's poem, "*The Road Not Taken*," I believe exemplifies where I am today. When the character says, "*I took the (road) least traveled, and it made all the difference,*" this line placed me at a point to review opportunities taken and missed, to reflect upon the road map of my past, and to recognize where I am in my life: *Do I want to stay with what is safe, or become a risk taker? How can I combine what I love to do with work, and still enjoy it?*

"Why didn't you follow the road in the first place," one might ask. My reasoning is this: I made a detour to do something "reliable, secure, safe". As a divorced mother, raising my son, I wanted to create a solid foundation for him regardless of what was happening in our surroundings. Thus, I *reacted* to my environment, instead of *responding*. Now, I choose to respond, with my eyes open and focused, I choose to take a risk. Allowing my aspirations to linger by the roadside, a victim, regardless of the choices made and taken in life, is no longer acceptable. I finally chose to no longer react to my circumstances, but to respond. I had a chance to meet an awesome man of God named Greg Powe, Senior Pastor of Revealing Truth Ministries, and in his series, *Big Vision, Big Provision*, he says, *"Don't let your present circumstances or situations re-define who God says you are."* That was powerful to me because I recognized that I had let others define me. Now, I am allowing God to redefine me.

I have always been intrigued with education and learning. I believe the meaning of my name is a result of this. It imparted into my spirit a thirst, a quest for knowledge and empowered me with strength for learning. I believe education can alter an individual's life, affect one's identity, and serve as a momentum for life's pursuit.

In the process of discovering my belief, I also recognized two other things one of which was how far away God seemed at this time, and the other was the discovery of the women in my family tree. During this time of my life it was the loneliest. As I stated earlier I felt like God was far away, just as I was beginning to think that I truly mattered to Him. Slowly, I realized that I had become like a demanding child, wanting my way; and yet, if I knew that if I truly loved God I would rather have it His way instead.

The second thing was the discovery about myself led me to look at the women in my family tree. All of them were strong, independent women, but they missed out on one thing . . . pursuit of purpose. I looked closer at my grandmothers (maternal and paternal) and my mother.

As I recalled a particular childhood memory about my maternal grandmother, what came to mind was her facial expression as she was "trying" to date. She had been divorced from my grandfather for several years and was trying to get back into the swing of things. As I look back at it now, I realize her heart was not in it, because she had already given it to my grandfather – lock, stock and barrel – as they used to say. Her husband and her children had become her life. As I looked closer still I saw she had the potential to be a great woman of God. Upon the death of my paternal grandmother, my sisters and I found out she wrote poetry and had a very sensitive side to her, which was seldom displayed. We found a note written by her, which served as a reflection of her ability to be hurt and frustrated. My mother died in her late forties. She spoke often of her dreams and desires, of the things she desired to do for the Lord. She was in the process of pursuing her purpose, and ended up not fulfilling it.

All of them were powerful, passionate women, yet they were limited! They ceased being who they were ordained to be because they lost themselves. I believe they went to their graves full of untapped potential. They went with something that was yearning to break free, but the barricades that kept them hostage were much stronger than their desire to take up the pursuit of purpose. However, they were at a major disadvantage: they had not been taught or encouraged to pursue their purpose, nor were they exposed to the level of teaching that we have today.

God used this powerful scenario to show me the potential of each one of these women lies within me! He showed me my potential is tied to their legacy. I had been handed the reins, now what choice would I make – pursue purpose or die unfulfilled, untapped? See, my Sisters, God is handing you the reins. What will you choose?

I no longer desired to keep reinventing myself for others. I desired to see the power of lasting, solid relationships with others and myself. This became my promise from God. Coming from a background of brokenness, I understand the need for wholeness.

God has positioned me to be guided in understanding, not only the meaning of cultural uniqueness of family relationships, but also to come into an awareness of how people interact with this uniqueness and how they incorporate this into their realities and their environments. Now that I have an understanding of this crucial part of the process, I am eager to learn and interact, and have a willingness to make a contribution to the community, as well as venture down paths yet undeveloped. I believe I will be presented with the opportunities to use the talents I have and cultivate new ones.

This statement from Thomas Merton's *No Man Is An Island*, sums up this book. He says:

> *"Why do we have to spend our lives striving to be something we would never want to be, if we only knew what we wanted? Why do we waste our time doing things which, if we only stopped to think about them, are just the opposite of what we were made for? We cannot be ourselves unless we know ourselves. But self knowledge is impossible [when] thoughtless and automatic activity keeps our souls in confusion . . . We cannot begin to know ourselves until we can see the real reasons why we do the things we do. It is not necessary that we succeed in everything. A man can be perfect and still reap no fruit from his work . . ."*

My sisters, in order to dream again and fulfill those dreams, we must begin to search for who we really are meant to be. We must be willing to see the "real reasons" why we do not pursue our dreams, why we do not pursue what rightfully belongs to us! We should no longer shortchange ourselves, which in turn shortchanges those around us, those we love most. Just like those around us, our dreams, our desires do matter and have a place in life.

Earlier I began to talk about my pursuit of purpose for my life. Well, now, I believe I have found it. As I began to experience a yearning to change, I realized I had allowed myself to be paralyzed by society's quota of having a secure job, not to mention my lack of confidence in myself, my lack of confidence in God.

Moreover, I found I wanted God to give me a sign, like a written guarantee from Him that this would work, and I would be successful if I pursued my dream. Basically, I wanted a guarantee from Him that I would not fail. I admit it. I let the fear of the unknown, as well as fear that I would lack the strength to complete this journey into the life I desired become a hindrance to me.

I struggled so, because I was aching so badly to do what was in me, but I did not know how to get it out. However, I started out trying to accomplish my vision as someone else, and not who I was created to be. I wanted to be content with my view of how God made me, but in my eyes what I wanted could not be conceived in my perception of myself. Thank God, I was wrong! God had to teach me that my vision was to be a vehicle of devotion and communication to do His work and to do it as myself, and not pretend I was someone else. I wanted to utilize my gifts and talents to bring God glory!

There is an importance, which lies in being comfortable in your own skin. Become content with being yourself, because there will always be something wrong with someone else's skin. The best part of my stumbling to find and fulfill my dream is that I found out God is patient with me and though I screw up, He will patiently wait for me, guiding me and loving me.

Susan L. Taylor, the Editorial Director of *Essence* Magazine does a segment in each issue titled *"In The Spirit."* In one particular article this phrase caught my eye. Ms. Taylor was talking about *The Everyday Sacred,* in it she says:

> "*Contentment and joy don't come from titles, trinkets or the toys we crave, but from being at peace with what is – whatever we're doing, wherever we are, whoever we're with. With practice we can make that mental shift. As God's highest creation, we can choose how we be.*"

What this says to me is success comes with the freedom to be us. It is not necessary for me to be someone other than who I am to achieve my highest goals. **What is necessary is for me to be who I really am, in order for me to be a success?**

As I look over my life at the choices and changes I have made, I have no regrets now. I have many people you have judged me and questioned whether or not I heard from God. Many have said to me, if you had done this or did that you would have a steady job. Maybe yes, maybe no, but I would be miserable just like those who are trying to keep me in the box by their way or society's way of thinking. My desire is to live life on the highest level possible, being who God created me to be, and giving to everyone He directs my way.

Remember, you are the key to turning your dream in your life into a reality. Be prepared to have God reveal where you are going, learn to embrace where you have been and stand strong for criticisms, negativism and praise, which will come your way.

My pastor, Dr. Stephen Rathod said at the close of a service one day, "*Do not let your memories become more than your dreams. Do not give up hope!*" I want to encourage you not to give up hope. To take a gigantic leap of faith and chose to live with hope that your dreams shall come to pass; to make a conscious decision to no longer live in the land of what-ifs.

Be bold my Sisters, life is a challenge to rise to, above and beyond our limitations, a challenge to grow and continue growing. I believe that every person is here for a purpose and sometimes we do not understand what it is. God has special plans for us and the plans are something that will leave a legacy. Turn your wills and your lives over totally to the God who cares for you, knowing that you do matter to Him.

My prayer is that as your days go, so shall your strength be. I encourage you to begin the journey to dream again, love again, live again, and know that my prayers and blessings are with you. So, take the risks my Sisters, it is well worth it!

Unlock Your Soul

The time has come, for you to no longer run,
And face the future as it unfolds.
The time has come for you to search yourself,
And unlock your soul.

The pain runs deep,
The mountain looks so steep,
There will be times, that it is hard to climb,
But just dig in and breathe again,
As in your search for yourself, you'll find.

You have looked high,
And you have looked low,
You have walked many paths,
Some crooked and slow,
Some fast and on a roll.

You have made some right turns,
And some wrong turns,
Some good choices,
And some bad ones.

You have lived and loved,
Cheated and been cheated on,
You have been faithful,
You have been unfaithful,
You have hurt, and been hurt,
You have cried, drank, laughed,
You have thrown up, had hangovers,

Been friends, liars, lovers, but most of all,
You have been sisters.

It is time to unlock that which is within,
And learn to live, laugh, and love again.

It is time to unlock your soul,
And let your spirit grow,
Let it soar to heights unknown,
Never to be caged again.
My sister, it is time to unlock your soul.

- *Java L. Collins*

Recommended Reading

Angelou, Maya. (1993). *Wouldn't Take Nothing For My Journey Now*. New York: Random House.

Barrett-Browning, Elizabeth. (1932). *Sonnets from the Portuguese*. New York: Harper.

Brown, Les. (1993). *Live Your Dreams*. New York: HarperCollins.

Buscaglia, Leo. (1978). Personhood: *The Art of Being Fully Human*. Videorecording. Thorafare, New Jersey: C. B. Slack/KVIE Sacramento, CA.

Cleage, Pearl. (1997). *What Looks Like Crazy On An Ordinary Day*. New York: Avon Books.

Collins, Java. (2003). *My Journey: The Beauty of the Valley*. Philadelphia, PA: Cornerstone Publishing.

Cowan, Connell (Dr.) & Kinder, Melvyn (Dr.). (1987). *Women Men Love, Women Men Leave*. New York: Distributed by Crown Publishers.

Hock, Dee. (1999). Fast Company, July/August 1999.

Jaffe, Lewis. (2000). Generations (by Erika Germer). Fast Company, June 2000.

Jakes, T.D. (1998). *The Lady, Her Lover and Her Lord*. New York: G. P. Putnam's Sons/Penguin Putnam, Inc.

McNaron, Toni A. H. (1985). *The Sister Bond: A Feminist View of a Timeless Connection*. New York: Pergamon Press.

Merton, Thomas. (1955). *No Man Is An Island.* Garden City, New York: Image Books/The Abbey of Our Lady of Gethsemane/Harcourt Brace (Orlando, FL).

Milton, John. (1992). *Paradise Lost.* New Jersey: Prentice Hall.

Montgomery, Ph.D., Dan. (1996). *Beauty In The Stone.* Nashville, Tennessee: Thomas

Nelson, Inc. Publishers.

Taylor, Susan. (2003). *The Everyday Sacred.* Essence Magazine, 2003.

Tompkins, Iverna. (1978). *The Worth of a Woman.* Plainfield, New Jersey: Logos International.

Proverbs 31

Song of Solomon

About the Author

Java L. Collins, MHR, is a dynamic woman of God; born in Coffeyville, Kansas and reared in Tulsa, Oklahoma. She is a gifted and talented author, speaker, and educator, who hold degrees in Education, Liberal Arts, Psychology, and Human Relations. In searching for the answers to life's numerous questions and challenges, Ms. Collins became a *"God chaser"* before realizing that God was unveiling her true destiny. Ms. Collins' goal is to use all that she has learned in her profession, education, and personal life experiences to teach, counsel, and empower others, especially women, to a more fulfilling and godly lifestyle.

Ms. Collins comprehends her purpose is to minister to women and men about the healing virtue and restoration power of God, through writing, the prophetic, dance, drama and prayer. She has developed an understanding of brokenness, a heart for healing and restoring through the power of God, which is necessary to reach wholeness. She believes *"you are a whole person going somewhere and about to accomplish something."* Ms. Collins knows that she has been called by God to *set the captives free* with her writings, but she also knows the reality of that is *as the heart cries, it speaks,* but who is willing to listen to its aches and tears to find answers? It is the desire of her heart that these writings minister to all who read them, setting free the dream within.

Ms. Collins currently resides in Tulsa, Oklahoma, and is a member of Covenant Family Church. She has a son, Milton Ramos, Jr.

To order a copy of this book please go to:

www.CornerstonePublishing.com

Excerpt from the author's upcoming books:

A Hole In My Soul: My Father's Sin

"Further reflection of my life led me to a startling
realization, The denial of my inheritance. Being a
bastard child, often puts one in the position of being
unable to claim one's natural inheritance as well as
any spiritual one. I began to focus on how not knowing
my rights as a natural daughter ran parallel to not knowing
my rights as a spiritual daughter, God's daughter."

A Hole in My Soul: My Father's Sin - It is a growing epidemic that fathers are no longer in the home for whatever cause. This gap is creating a negative effect both naturally and spiritually. This is a book for every person whose father has left or is gone and they feel like there is something missing. Like they have a hole in a part of them, a "hole" in their soul that needs to be filled so that they can move on as a "whole" person. This book allows us to investigate and ask questions that some wish we would leave alone, but asking the questions and dealing with them will help bolster you to change and become all that you can for the glory of God, sealing the hole as you become whole.

A Hole in My Soul: My Father's Sin offers an autobiographical work about the author as she continues on her passage to become whole.

My Journey: The Beauty of the Valley

My Journey: The Beauty of the Valley: a 4-part collection of poetic and prophetic psalms. So often we get tied up physically, emotionally and spiritually when things aren't going our way, and these distractions create an imbalance in us, which leaves in its quake a wondering about who we are, why me, etc.

My Journey begins to deal more with worshipping God, regardless of where you are in life, regardless of the situations and circumstances. It puts into practice speaking the word, in season and out, to bring us hope, life and love. This book reflects upon the complexity of emotions we feel, but more so it directs how we feel towards God. It brings us to an awakening in ourselves of who God is and trying to see Him as Father, while making the journey towards spiritual transformation, self –discovery and finding fulfillment in God and His Word. He gives us the reassurance that He has been there all the time.

1739736